THE DOVE OF THE MORNING NEWS

THE TEST SITE POETRY SERIES

Claudia Keelan, University of Nevada, Las Vegas, *Series Editor*

The Test Site Poetry Series is a collaboration between the University of Nevada, Las Vegas's Black Mountain Institute, *Witness* and *The Believer,* and the University of Nevada Press. Each year, the series editor along with an advisory board, which includes Sherwin Bitsui, Donald Revell, Sasha Steensen, and Ronaldo Wilson, will select a winner and a runner-up. The selected winners will be published by the University of Nevada Press as part of this series.

Winning books engage the perilous conditions of life in the twenty-first century, as they pertain to issues of social justice and the earth. They demonstrate an ethos that considers the human condition in inclusive love and sympathy, while offering the same in consideration with the earth.

Refugia
Kyce Bello

Riddle Field
Derek Thomas Dew

Mouth of the Earth
Sarah P. Strong

A Sybil Society
Katherine Factor

Interior Femme
Stephanie Berger

Joyful Orphan
Mark Irwin

The Reckoning of Jeanne d'Antietam
Matthew Moore

The Dove of the Morning News
Bruce Bond

Rain, Wind, Thunder, Fire, Daughter
H. G. Dierdorff

The Dove of the Morning News

POEMS

Bruce Bond

UNIVERSITY OF NEVADA PRESS | *Reno & Las Vegas*

University of Nevada Press | Reno, Nevada 89557 USA
www.unpress.nevada.edu
Copyright © 2024 by Bruce Bond
All rights reserved

Manufactured in the United States of America

Cover design by Caroline Dickens
Cover photograph © by iStock, enginakyurt11

Library of Congress Cataloging-in-Publication Data
Names: Bond, Bruce, 1954- author.
Title: The dove of the morning news : poems / Bruce Bond.
Description: Reno : University of Nevada Press, [2024] | Summary: "In poems
  both personal and historical, *The Dove of the Morning News* explores
  conceptions of collectivity, inflected by each psyche, as a force of both
  connection and division." Provided by publisher.
Identifiers: LCCN 2024008398 | ISBN 9781647791735 (paperback) | ISBN
  9781647791742 (ebook)
Subjects: LCGFT: Poetry.
Classification: LCC PS3552.O5943 D68 2024 | DDC 811/.54—dc23/
  eng/20240402
LC record available at https://lccn.loc.gov/2024008398

ISBN 9781647791735
ISBN 9781647791742
LCCN: 2024008398

They have seen the vessel that was carrying us along.
They have marked the creaming of the bow wave.

—Pierre Teilhard de Chardin

Contents

THE DOVE OF THE MORNING NEWS

I.

Imperium

When I was small, I drew small people and gave to each the life

of the others, the sense of a solitary shared self that many make,

when gods above them flip the pages. I was learning how to think

of others when they are far away, to lay down a sketchpad of faces

in incremental variations, the closer the semblance of the moments

the stronger the illusion, the more fluid the movement of the lips.

And once, when I was small, a mother stepped out of the paper,

out of the steady brokenness that gives to each a silent language.

*

I was learning how to think of the self, not the self as the river I am

when I have yet to say *river* or *self* or *I am learning how to think.*

Not that kind but the chatter of a film projector, where I play a role,

a figure in an animated feature spooling in the basement of a brain.

The river you hear is no river, but the crackle of an old soundtrack.

Its crawl of fiction crumples as it turns. But the ache of light is real,

the way it suffers to be seen, heard, taken over. I think therefore I

fail the surplus of experience. The dark of whom is everything I love.

*

A child crawls in a hall with a mirror at the far end, and as the figure

in the mirror crawls a little closer, the child feels a little larger, darker.

With every move the child makes, so too the stranger whose shadow

trails into the hall in the mirror. If a shadow could stand, it would be

a monster. It would be a child who cries in pitches only dogs can hear.

And shiny objects with hearts of glass. And when the mirror shatters,

a monster would rise from the shards to see in them his brokenness.

He would kneel down like mist at dawn to give to each a child's name.

*

Long ago, a flock of blackbirds flew into one man's ear and turned
into a solitary figure. *Blackbird,* he whispered, and the bird flew away.
Just when he thought himself one of the family, he found his life
abandoned. When at last he woke, one of his eyes was gouged out.
Bird, he said, more bitterly this time. With every thought of the wound,
how it ate into the visual world, he saw the glossy jacket of the bird.
With every song, his blood turned cold. And when he woke again,
his eye returned, but everything he dreamed was bitter and black.

*

Begin with a four-year-old who spins a dial, and the needle falls

on orange or green. Then a gift, a shirt in the corresponding color.

Now ask the child to read cartoon figures in the same two shades,

unscripted scenes whose silence summons the prejudice of being

one of the fold. Orange versus green. That sideways glance. Is

it conspiratorial or shy. A shirt will tell you. Truth loves no one.

But dread has favorites. Its brain a child inside a brain that watches.

Like a wilderness some call bankable or pointless. Others, home.

*

I met a squirrel who came to my window every morning to be fed, and though I was never sure it was the same squirrel, I called him *squirrel* and loved him all the same. Him and his schizophrenic freeze-tag with voices in his head. The squirrel brain in me said, *Maybe you just love the love of squirrels,* and it was true. My email signature read, *yada, yada, PhD, lover of squirrels.* My motto was, *The good of the relation is something other than the good* within *it.* A squirrel told me that. *Take this,* I said, *a nut. Whoever you are.*

*

Frankenstein the creature will tell you, the volt that shocks the dead to life falls from clouds whose rage drifts in from the unseen story, like a mob in the making, waiting to explode. He will tell you, he is an animated figure, a lightning rod, a doll. Heaven strikes the nerve of what the frightened call a *monster,* and his eyes in ours are ours through which we see his father turn away. It will take a blind man to read the stapled lesions in a startled face. The proximity of touch will tell you. Forget what you heard. To relate belongs to one alone.

*

The cartoon animals who suffer the blows and explosives that move the plot along know what it is to be cast out of more serious creatures, like a language from the lips of mothers. They were born to survive, and we loved them for it, knowing they cannot touch us. Even as light died inside the chicken hawk, as the glass tube shattered and a ghost of gas lingered in the air, they taught our brokenness to rise. They mend like rivers. My mother's face was a river. The night she left this earth for the other, she was the mirror that moved as my face stood still.

*

In Bagdad once, a Mongol herd rounded up the priests and scholars,

cut their throats, and hurled them in the Tigris. It turned the water

to rust, the widows to water, eyes downstream to the littered shore.

Then to make a bridge, the invaders dumped wagonloads of books

that stained the current black. When a violence spreads, it scatters

the remnants of erasure. It scours faces of their features, out there,

where the story ends and ends. The lost manuscript will tell you.

A final chapter echoes through the others, because they are not here.

✻

It's alive, says the scientist whose unkempt hair stiffens into quills,

which tells you something is seriously wrong below, inside that head,

his pride afloat the danger music of his blood. *It,* the scientist says,

but what do we call the new human whose parts are old and aching.

If not *Lamp of Knowledge,* what. *Mania, Regret, No Son of Mine.*

No. The affair began with a fiction, but suffering is another matter,

and love needs a name. It needs a threshold, the way a hand needs

a shadow hand to lie down on, to press against the shadow of a face.

*

If you draw enough and talk and, in your talking, listen, you begin to light

the many apartments of a project on the margin. I too am worried, scared,

beaten by strangers I later punish in my dreams. I see in each the avatar

I cannot be, no stranger can, no tribe, no urchin who thinks in exaltations

of violence and cartoon. If, in some feature set inside a neighbor's kitchen,

you dab her open wound with a cloth, you understand, as lesions must,

the primacy of touch, that place the tremor of the lidded eye subsides.

But you are in there still. Like a thousand dark apartments. Like blood.

*

The face of many is one face, its eyes sewn shut. Its mouth gagged.

Its suffering a string that gathers followers like crystals. I have seen it.

I gave it the breath of a creature to whom the many are a stranger.

For though the face is blind, I see, in it, a mirror, the kind that calls

from the end of a long dark hall. Lonely as a monster or some such friend.

What I do not, cannot, know fills the pitchers of the grieved with blood.

And those who hang in the bayou break down into particles, frames, flies.

All night, they bronze the wind, they toll, waiting for the one to cut them down.

II.

Vellum

To make a sheet of vellum, you need a corpse.
> A cow will do, a sheep, a saint, a criminal
from some dark ward of the nineteenth century.

> The inside of the skin makes the finest surface
beneath the pen or press, the least familiar, least
>> plagued with scars, follicles, mementi mori.

You need lime to burn the nonsense and clarify
> the page, to make an opening around the word,
a kind of glass around the specimen you read,

> and if, as you open the doors of skin on books,
you hear the moan of cattle in the distance, remember.
> It is nothing. Only flesh. Longing to be heard.

*

Deep in this archive lies a book whose skin
        tombs the story no one lived to tell. No one
knows who died there, if they gave their body

        to science or God or no one in particular,
or if the first to hold it felt a sign, a pulse,
        did they feel their own in the part about soul,

how, as it leaves the body, it enters the afterlife
        of the reader's eye. And not just any reader,
but one who rereads and shares it with a friend,

        who binds it in her arms, beloved, as souls are
bound, released, and everywhere, in the fly
        and the fever, the flowing waters of the eye.

                        *

A boy shakes as he reads a poem about his father,
       how he found him in the basement with a rope
burn on his neck, and then the part about Escher

       who was not his father, not himself. Only a picture
of enclosure like a basement where the stairs flow
       up or down, depending on the tilt of your head.

If you find yourself looking at a boy, thinking
       of a rope and the scent of rain that salts the air,
consider Escher. Consider the interlocking cells

       of skin that hold us in, the world away, depending.
When you hear a tremor inside a song, think
       of thunder going down, and up, and spilling over.

*

Dear God, a girl writes with a finger on her leg,
        I am writing now in the phantom ink of touch
to tell you I am sorry. I have not written you

        in years. What can I say that you do not know.
You were there, I imagine, when my brother
        took me to the attic and did to me the thing

I cannot talk about, not now. I want to ask,
        what is a body to you, to the purified survivor
stepping through the gate. Is it what we throw

        off in horror, the once loved who then betrays us.
Tell me. Was it your body that suffered mine,
        yours in me I write against. And for. And to.

*

The boy with the cross tattooed on his back
        grows one inch, and the crucifix another,
as if he too were nailed to it, as it was nailed

        indelibly to him. It took patience to stitch,
let alone suffer a sacrifice that consuming,
        that consumed, haloed in blood, and bodiless,

its paraclete deposed, called the way a child
        calls a missing mother. To think of the burden
as his, he must first stand apart, as bodies do.

        Remember the moment the cord was cut. No one does.
He must see a missing body in the distance,
        the crossbeams of a window against his broken skin.

*

Once, I penned the number of a stranger in
          my palm, promising to call, as she too promised,
back when small talk was enough to raise the flag

          on some holiday picnic, but I never called,
never got my promise. I was a kid and scared
          of what I wanted in the stranger. In my palm.

And so I wrote in hidden places. My notebook
          was my other hand. I buried a boyhood there,
and the page went blue. Dirty words on men's

          room walls taught me, the body is everywhere
blue, abused, written over. *Shit,* I say when I
          am stung. *If you are lonely, call,* the wall replies.

*

The woman who touches the scar on her shoulder
       over and over is a friend of mine and listens
over coffee to me and the scar, and when she talks,

       she talks to her broken part, and it talks back.
Where it came from, she cannot say. Did a lamp fall
       or a wine glass shatter, hurled across the room.

She knows perhaps and does not know and sends her hand
       to look. But what she finds is a mother, alone,
who fell one day into a silence. And that was it,

       my friend says. Her mother never spoke again.
No cure, no explanation, no whisper to the daughter.
       Heavens no, not you. It has nothing to do with you.

*

The boy who passes out at a party and wakes,
        his face marked by the sharpies with another face,
will never see the whole picture, what others see.

        He will never look at both eyes inked against
his eyelids, how even as he sleeps, he wakes.
        Even as he dreams a second face descending.

a mask of attention stares as it must have once,
        the day the nib filled the surface of the pupil,
when it scored a frightened child on the far side.

        And sure, it fades. But sometimes still, he feels it.
Some nights a pair of eyes tears away from the bone.
        It floats into the dark and lies there and takes it.

                    *

I loved a woman once with a lover's name
        tattooed at the base of her neck, and I must
have kissed it in the dark, I will never know,

        I know only she suffered quietly to see it
in my eyes, how they held for her the bitterness
        joy breeds when it leaves you for another.

But the last thing I wanted was to wound her,
        to lay my head against a name I answered to.
How much better to be strange, to talk names

        with a darkened woman I knew and could not know
apart from how, long ago, I held her, how then,
        we broke, to bear the scars we could not bear alone.

*

The deep tissue work I get to make it through
        each week tells me where I keep punishing
myself, for what, I do not know, but I want

        to say, as if in explanation, the earth below
is burning. My therapist asks, does this hurt,
        and yes, it does, and so I say, deeper, please.

Which is when, in the starlight of my anguish,
        an angel appears with a gold sword and cuts
the knot in my back that weeps a river of blood.

        All good things begin in blood, she says, and I
say, thank you. I drink a lot of water. I begin
        again, spitting embers, learning how to breathe.

*

When I was a kid, I spotted a black swastika
        on another kid's wrist and felt a little scared,
the way he pulled his sleeve up to let me see

        then let it fall. Call it a threat, or invitation,
I could not tell, but what I saw was my own blood
        inked into a boy so ashamed and clueless

he stumbled over words and the laughter of class.
        We were kids and cruel and terrified of all
the wrong things, but now, when I think of him,

        I think of bones. I think of all I never see
in this body or that. I smell the smoke of hair
        plunged in a tunnel like an arm in a sleeve.

*

Tattooed numbers on the arms of survivors
      fade a little more each day and never quite
so long as blood runs its trains beneath the surface.

      Skin scatters to the winds its dead, the blue
we inhale as dust, never knowing whose.
      Which is why a young man goes to a tattoo

artist who studies a photo of a grandfather's arm
      and needles the same venous shade and sum
in a clearer font, as if the prick of entry

      passed a torch deep into the younger body,
into the eye that sees a sign somewhere inside
      the blood of inception, the sharpening wound.

*

Numbers do the dull work they set out to do.
　　　They say what they mean, long before history
with its bodies pressures numbers to say more.

　　　Always more. No matter the sum a body bears.
When I feel one press against my chest, I feel
　　　my ribcage rise. I call my number numberless.

It is a clear point of view in a mound of glasses.
　　　The shoe that fits in a motherload of shoes.
I knew a man who returned from so much death,

　　　he rarely spoke. If he wanted to talk of it,
that was his decision. And we honored that.
　　　We honored the silence that was his. And his alone.

*

To the death clerk with his books, I ask, why
       does it matter, this need to pin the horror down.
Why the colonnades of ledgers where bodies rise,

       to each a resting place, part of the larger order.
What imaginary reader comes to your side
       to find what is loved and lost among the records.

Does the ink of the instrument give you comfort.
       Do you dip the hollow tip in dreamless sleep.
Madness longs for an address. It fills asylums

       with those who count audibly to no one now.
But the sum is always nothing. The sum of all
       bound in skin. Because you wanted it to last.

*

Beneath this page lies the body of a child
      who survives. Every seven years, the new
generation of cells comes. A now exhausted

      skin hangs on the armature that goes unseen.
Our history's angel is everywhere incarnate.
      Invisible you who sit before me at the table.

In your eye lies the dark mountain at my back.
      Or in my eye. For all I know. Once I admit
what I can never see in you, my body softens,

      but the talk goes on. The silent armature
inside a word goes a little farther. The stench
      beyond the razor wire, drifting through the village.

*

Where books are burned, one day, men, I read that.

Then the book closed so that I might open it,
asleep. I might open my spectacles and stare

at nothing, as if a burning nothingness were there.
Millions get their news from an angry man.

The wider his eye the less it sees. But who am I.

I could be reading anger where there is only greed,

the blistered sap of it that spits into the camera.
I learned from an autocrat who moves his hands

a lot on stage, all you need is one dull hammer
to strike a nerve. You could gun a man and walk.

You could set yourself ablaze and holler, *fire, fire.*

*

Once the führer put a bullet through his lover
      and then his head, many wept by their radios;
a great blur fell; leaflets appeared on city walls,

      photos of the camps, and everything felt unreal,
each page a postcard from the end of the world.
      Wind lifted the victims from the mortar and char

and set them down, and the wind was no longer wind,
      flesh not flesh but a wire doll draped in plaster.
Was it just last week the generals in their bunker

      eyed a model of the führer's home in the future.
Where to put the heroes' ashes, they wondered,
      where the joy ride with its pony, gashed with steel.

*

In the acupuncture star chart of the hand,
        the tip of the index finger corresponds
to the hand it is on, like a constellation

        of the god of stars who thinks of them and lo,
a god appears. The image of a smaller hand
        thimbles the finger that grows a finger of its own.

Does the echo ever end, the fractal of stars
        inside the cell, and inside every star, an eye.
If I think small enough, will I ever glimpse

        the big picture. If I kneel to a father's grave,
will I see the many, will my fingers close
        the lid that takes with it the darkness and the stars.

*

I have written into a pair of glasses the word
        love on one lens, *hate* on the other, like a prisoner
does on the hands he uses to defend himself.

        Most of what I see is ink. And walls that strike.
My father struck me once, I do not know why.
        If he were alive, I would remove my glasses

and ask him for a story. It is hard now.
        His tongue is broken. Most of what I hear is ink.
But he loves a story, so I nod now and then.

        I could be an important part and never know.
I could hear myself walking through the wall
        of a room in a man. And never want to leave.

*

Those who suffer a condition called skin writing
      or dermagraphia know the slightest scratch will
raise welts in the language of incidental touch.

      But you can choose to write it with your finger.
You can see across the page a cursive surface,
      as each word must when new, when without notice

the disinherited stray comes scratching at your door.
      Especially at night, when self-affliction is the worst.
Blood grows predisposed to enter the conversation.

      Thus the discomfort that makes sleep so critical
and hard. But if you go deep, the writing fades.
      If you pierce the bone, the written cannot follow.

*

Too late, too soon, a little of both, a lot of neither.
      When does a mother answer to the child's finger
laid against the numbers. Blue. As the veins

      that bear her cells away, and still the mark is blue.
Children pry, they must, they wander in the garden,
      and the earth on the margins opens up a hole.

I have seen it. I have heard a silence in the shape
      of a bird fly into a chimney and, years later, appear
with a scrap of newsprint, a hair, a tooth, a small

      gold shoelace for a nest. Anything to make a future.
I have watched the pages of the numbered fall
      into a mother's lap, and the earth remembers.

III.

Cross

In the painting of a ship called *Helen,*
       named for the love of the man who built it,
the mainsail tells you there are lives below.
       When I close my eyes, it moves so far
and never farther, just a painting after all

       whose liberties are ancient. Impossible
to tell the seer from the seen, the artist
       from the far side of the portrait, the merchant
liner dry-docked, years ago, or drowned
       beneath the down-surge of a silent cry.

When I close my eyes, I know a ship
       is out there, in *the world,* I say, a word
I use for this traffic of circumstances
       in which I lose the wind in the winded,
the eye in the eyed, the mast in the amber

       of the brush whose charity of attentions
sweeps away the details of the rigging.
       I know so little of ships, outside this
desire to sail and remain on shore to watch.
       The world, I say. Is lonely for the world.

My student asks, do I think people will
       ever get better, not this one or that alone,
but a culture. And since our *culture* is
       invisible and everywhere, as currents are
beneath the vivified portraits of the deep

       from any one perspective, I see a ship.
And on that ship, a mother with child.
       I want to say to my student, yes, or no,
or I wish I knew, or let's start again.
       With a watching over, a ship, a child.

When the tear gas clatters to my feet,
          I hear a hiss of waves where there are none.
I see the woman gesture for her daughter
          toward an island in the New York harbor,
the chill of fog burning off the surface.

          I want to ask, do you feel safe, held.
Do you see things from the child's eyes
          and know you cannot. Do you ache in waves
across the threshold, as you did when you
          arrived, speechless, bathed in a mother's blood.

I want to say that cruelty is *systemic,*
          that I too speak a dialect of symptoms
I know or not. Either way, a symptom.
          I was born unsafe. The accent spread.
Child mimics child, painting paintings,

          ship ships, in the wake of any one
craft the bow of another. Long before
          the desert fathers, I am thinking there were tribes.
Some music maybe. One voice, then another.
          Only the essentials to survive.

Long ago I learned to speak because
          the world was just too close or far away.
Too silent or full or likely to forget.
          A game where faces reappear taught
my dread to laugh. Laughter was the nonsense

          that blazed a path for the other voices.
As others leave, sometime still the laughter.
          When my mother left the room, I left
my flesh to follow her. I became her
          shadow's shadow and stepped inside her steps.

It starts here, I think, the metaphysics
of the missing and beloved, the desire
to be better, by which I mean, a part.
I knew a woman who put a steak knife
through her son's tongue, *come here,* she said

in a voice made small and harmless, *here.*
For the boy, it was a mystery and more so
as he turned away. Cruelty is frightened.
As am I. When I wake, I live in a city no
farther away than the dream I am leaving.

When I think of architectural abuse,
I think of one such place, one such city.
I see a conspiracy of nightmares now.
I see a flock return to the tree
as one returns the wounding to a wound.

A child counts on her fingers, *one, one,*
and the sound goes on, because she is
not well, not one at all, she is no child.
Only an abstract of experience,
a portrait hung in a room gone blind.

When I see a black crucifix haloed
in red across a uniform or banner,
I see a bombed cathedral in Berlin,
in the breeze the ghost of salt, meat,
little flags on sale, the train that brought me here

gaining speed in the opposite direction.
At the altar, a cross welded out of nails,
spikes salvaged from a chapel overseas.
When I enter an emptiness whose ceiling
breathes, I lift my gaze like an anchor.

I look down at a boy on the street, asleep,
      his hand against his eyes in the sun.
How he does it, I do not know, how the dream
      survives the traffic that would crush it.
Is his sleeping dreamless and waking mad.

      What is that line of smoke in the distance
if not a furnace. An unforeseen disaster.
      Or a signature forged of airborne ashes,
the ghost of the ghost of the sternum
      of the mast. A cross afloat the sail on fire.

IV.

The Dove of the Morning News

Click on Pierre Teilhard de Chardin,
and you find a man whose Christ has a body,
and that body is not finished growing.

The surface of modern earth lies below
a glow of talk and optic fiber, the angel
of our noosphere, engorged and breathing,

metastasized into intelligent machines,
the throes of fevers arcing our backs,
contagions of our traffic raised, curved,

shuttled through the crossed emergent roar
of light. You see what de Chardin saw,
our circuits cast in one great nervous system

of the whole, flags of contrails flowing over
cities, the blood of strangers into streams
of smoke that flood the boundaries we call strange.

*

What is the will to live if not the means
and meaning of the bridge, what if not
a common fire beneath the stanchions,

the sharp green scent of a burst of rain.
Yesterday my wife fainted in the market.
She shattered her bottles, broke her jaw,

and the many strangers rushed to her
to offer her bandages, an ambulance call,
the wordless reparation of her groceries.

Without the mask or glove of our season,
an old man knelt in his boy-blue super-
market vest, and she said, thank you, please,

do not touch me. She can feel it still,
that hand. When she lies down, it lies down
beside her. Like a beast beside a child.

*

What good is our proximity to heaven
if it sends no word. Only the winds
of Chernobyl over northern Europe,

the air that binds, empties what it fills,
fevers the autumns of New England
like a plague. What you cannot see

you see in the eyes of the paralyzed,
the drift of the garbage, the uplifted
hair and banners on the white house lawn.

You hear it in our cattle like a train
to somewhere, though no one says just where.
And you know it will not last, the air

for the taking, but you were born to it,
for the cry to clear your lung of spit
and blood, to search the right words to breathe.

*

After bombs beat the many precincts
of our town to cinders, the charred bricks
stood in jagged monoliths or scattered

across the roads that carried us survivors
by foot. In search of what, hard to tell,
the living, the dead, the unknown neighbor.

After the weary initiation of repairs,
as the wreckage cooled and peace received
its signatures, a chill swept over us,

a shared sense of what we suffered, lost,
what we saw in the random casualty.
The deep sensation of the irrevocable

haunted small greetings among strangers.
Blood banks drained, and filled, and filled again.
When one eye shuddered, so too another.

*

The earth below the throat is paradise,
said a child of the age of permission,
and I worried, I called, and then, he died

of the shame and sacrament he drank,
alone, divided against the voice that says,
you can love a heaven and hate its god.

You can vacate the house and chronic
rancor of your childhood and pause,
look up, hypnotized beneath the white

glass of trees, not knowing what it is
you know. *I cannot quite recall,* we say,
speaking on behalf of a fog that floats

rock, silk, and heroin across the ocean.
I cannot, says the wind, or some lost soul
who walks the earth, never touching down.

*

Where a mind divides, so too a hood
or national prayer breakfast where the word
love becomes a matter of contention.

We were born, after all, into the flesh
whose mission, like a meal, reminds us:
eat, sleep, tweet, do what you must do

to live. Like a gerrymandered district
or parish of dollars earmarked for promotion.
Small wonder we look up from pancakes

and prayer in disbelief at our poor choices.
I too feel lost, listening for the danger,
like any bank or church or living thing.

I feel this new and quiet desperation
enter the room, if only to whisper, *here
I am*. Like a phantom limb, *here, here.*

*

I love the tenor of talk in the morning
café where I drink mine black and read,
in the news, that scientists have found

a little cavern in the word *whole,*
it was there all along, unlike its cousin
complete, the entire room now full

of mouths opening and closing and if
you look down a throat, deep, you see
the shadow of the person in the name

and in the friend, once, whose pain was
so singular the doctors could not get
their scope past the scarring of the wine.

They could not tunnel to the issue, and so
he sighed, relieved, his whole body relaxed,
then fell back into darkness once again.

When I find our congregation online,
a swastika sprayed across the playground,
I know, the new proximities are here.

The velocity of money and bad ideas
feeds a conflagration of stars, crosses,
fast machines and plows them into crowds.

I too lost a friend in Pittsburg to talk
so deadly it turned into a man, a creature
of garbled anger in the chatroom dark.

The new proximities travel at the speed
of bullets stripped of jackets and the chamber,
the new noosphere an aurora of texts

around a planet that does what planets do,
what bodies do when a stranger enters
shul to wipe the faces from their bones.

*

Dear puritans of a perfect social order,
I too have felt distracted at the party
that is, granted, one imperfect space.

Ever the guy who reddens with important
views, or waxes on about their dull
vacation, but hey, we are forgiving here,

a bit messed up and grateful to be safe.
Policemen of the human heart, thank you.
You deserve a break, so take one. Please.

I will remember fondly your vigilance.
I will see myself in you, and then. I won't.
Because we are just unspeakably different

and lay our sacks of skin into dreams
that are genuine, odd, or odd enough
to reach the unheard voice and whisper, *yes.*

*

The pursuit of happiness makes time
a blur of consequences, as heaven is
for one believer, and utopia for others.

In other words, an idea, like a house:
in this life, we say. Or *are you happy,*
when it feels small to answer, *yes* or *no.*

Tonight, I learned a great woman died,
a nurse who caught the fever of a patient,
and I wonder how she felt about a world

she left untouched, unfinished and afraid.
Every day will be the one she missed,
the deed undone, the calling she passed on.

Every year will bring the hour she changed
the bedpan of another, in a white room
called happiness, in which she disappears.

*

Here, between abysses of enormity
and the quantum small, a child is born.
A figure so intricate we cannot see

where matter ends, life begins, a body
stands to walk from evolution's flow chart
into a room, late, with a table, a lamp,

a sheet of paper, a hearth for the fire
to lay the skeletons of last night's dream.
The new sublime is a place like this,

an abyss that eats the sun and grass.
I have traveled a great distance to arrive
here, in this garden of black flowers, to say,

I am sorry, to the widow on behalf
of no one, nothing, everything, death,
the part gone speechless for whom I speak.

*

The abyss of synthesis, de Chardin
called it, the dark and darker labyrinth
you see wherever you see life, as if,

through the lens of a new science set
to music, we could fall in love again,
revive, in our basilica of nerves,

the marriage of mind to some first star,
here, in a coffee shop named *Aura.*
An abyss of design so fine, it opens up

the O's of awe in holy counterpoint.
But what of the maze that lies there still
when the eye closes. The veil of flies

descends. Cats wander the empty house.
What of the kilowatt that cannot kick
a stone-white heart back into the world.

*

When I first saw the Sistine Chapel,
I saw a great room inside a smaller.
I saw a god inside the need for god,

and so, one man, high in the scaffolds,
on his back and painting the flesh tones
of lovers into us, their afterlife.

I took them home, reimagined them
whenever I speak of gods and angels.
Call paradise a bridge over waters

in whom the shadows of the girders float
and lay a cooler weather on the river.
I too have received that from a stranger.

I have heard a radio playing in a far
room a cheerful and infectious tune,
though I cannot find that room, not yet.

*

Dear philosopher of the noosphere,
I love you. And I worry about the axis
of pure white light driven through the planet,

how we breathe it when we whisper: *love.*
I want to believe in the evolution
of kindness, that it grows more and more

complex in its affections for the strange.
The problem with paradise is the one
good bar where each is every, plus one.

But we live in uncertain times. Therefore
tyrants, purges, plagues that quarantine
our angels. Yes, I know. You are dead.

But stay in touch. All that is beautiful
bespeaks a bit of chaos. Text me. Call.
For we are different, thank the stars. Between us.

*

When Lao bid farewell to Confucius,
he said, *Friend, go easy on the dogma.*
Remember, laws create the criminal.

But if laws are bad, what of the lawless
precincts of criminals at war, the lions
at heart who unhinge the prison gate.

Precisely, said Lao, *the mind at war.*
What of the bitter narcissist in office,
the bully, the baby, the wall, the eternal

disappointment who could not please his father.
Seek the lowest places, Lao said.
Be like the river as it falls. And then

he left. And between philosophers,
a tenderness opened. A prison filled.
The blood of millions wandered to the sea.

*

*No evolutionary future awaits except
in association with everyone else.* I read
that once. I was hoping for a picture.

I was hoping for a speaker just close
enough, in the sweet spot of the seen.
The icon of my Christ links to Virgil

to Jove. The spirit of each is none alone.
Like earth that way, aflame in the eyes
of machines, and our eyes looking back.

When I look back, when de Chardin looks
my way, I feel a little powerless,
pointless, like clicking *like* beside a fact,

as if it needs me. It needs more friends
and feels nothing. No favorite, no cold.
I google *everyone,* and my cursor freezes.

*

To touch the untouchable, our hands,
invisibly inked, pressed into a record
no one reads, each anonymous labor,

each microscopic kindness or mistake,
scattered in one continuous departure,
is this what we want, to be everywhere

and nowhere, always dissolving, always
arriving, leaving like faces in the mirrors
of the nursing home. Always in the air,

ashes from a mountain, long repressed,
falling as a coastal rain, without sound,
and you feel it, smell it, the small winged

consequence of everything, and nothing
untainted, undisturbed, and the smoke
in your eye turns to water, and you follow.

*

Long ago, de Chardin dreamt he would
die one Easter, and, indeed, he did.
He loved the iconography of ending

with a question. And a room of heads
would nod to hear a query rise, like balloons
across an April lawn in the silence after.

But that is another story. What I mean
to say is: he was talking with a friend.
Before he died, he reddened with wine,

toasting time as a journey toward a chat
like this. And then his arm went numb.
His chest ached. His friend got up to catch

the man who fell like a dime in a fountain.
It was just that quick, and like a friend,
the whole sky broke. And took the silver in.

*

Something for the ferry, for the moon
laid down across the eyelid of the sun.
Something for the garden to comfort

the beloved arranged in neighborhoods
named for the faith of lives who visit.
Something for a name engraved against

the quiet of the yard, the hollow place
burrowed through the halo of the grass.
Something for those who wait for the rest

of night to carve its passage and withdraw.
Some grief is slow to make its way in,
slower still to fade. How strange this gift,

this earth we leave the moment that we enter,
this pain so deep it feels no pain, not yet,
this stone that breaks the circle of the sun.

*

Most of what we dream is dreamless.
A window on an emptiness, a womb
of stars. Who can tell us otherwise.

Long ago my mother lay quietly dying
beneath the dove of the morning news.
We came together, my sisters, my brother,

me. We were confused like the rooms
of Los Angeles when the power goes,
when streetlamps sink into one black pool.

We slept, if we slept, in shifts, laughed
the odd, cautious laughter of the grieving.
But I recall a distance among us, unlike

all others. Something my mother said,
when I was not listening. And it just kept
calling, small and trembling. Like a star.

Acknowledgments

The author would like to thank the editors of the following journals who first published these poems: *Alaska Review, Colorado Review, Interim,* and *Meridian.* Also a thanks to the editors of *Meridian* for selecting "Vellum" for the *Meridian Editor's Prize in Poetry.*

About the Author

BRUCE BOND is the author of thirty-five books including, *Patmos, Behemoth, Liberation of Dissonance,* and *Invention of the Wilderness,* plus two books of criticism: *Immanent Distance,* and *Plurality and the Poetics of Self.* He has received numerous honors including the Juniper Prize, the Elixir Press Poetry Award, the New Criterion Prize, two Texas Institute of Letters Best Book of Poetry awards, a National Endowment for the Arts fellowship, and seven appearances in *Best American Poetry.* Bond teaches part time as a Regents Emeritus Professor of English at the University of North Texas.